Animal Signatures

Edward Claridge
and Betty Ann Milligan

Nimbus Publishing &
The Nova Scotia Museum
Halifax, Nova Scotia, 1992

95 96 97 98 7 6 5 4 3

Produced as part of the Nova Scotia Museum
Program of the Department of Education,
Province of Nova Scotia

Minister: Honourable Guy J. Le Blanc
Deputy Minister: Armand F. Pinard

First edition published by
the Nova Scotia Museum 1976

Second edition 1977

Third edition 1984

Fourth edition, revised and re-designed,
co-published by the Nova Scotia Museum
and Nimbus Publishing Limited, 1992

A product of the Nova Scotia Government
Co-publishing Program

Illustrated by: Ed Claridge
Design by: Jay Rutherford
Layout by: David H. MacDonald
Cover Photo by: John Sherlock
Printed by: McCurdy Printing & Typesetting Limited

Produced by the Department of Supply & Services
and the Nova Scotia Museum

Canadian Cataloguing in Publication Data

Claridge, Edward

Animal signatures
(Field guide series)

Co-published by the Nova Scotia Museum
ISBN 1-55109-048-1

1. Animal Signatures–Identification. I. Milligan, Betty Ann. II. Nova Scotia Museum. III. Title. IV. Series: Field guide series (Halifax, N.S.)

QL768.C52 1993 599.09715 C92-098730-3

Contents

How To Use This Book

This field guide has been prepared as an introduction to animal signs found in Nova Scotia. No attempt has been made to make it complete. Rather, we have depicted the most commonly encountered animals and their signs. Increasing your knowledge of the animal life of the province will increase the pleasure you get from going for a walk. If you become an enthusiast you can obtain further information on Nova Scotia wildlife from the reference books listed at the back of the book.

The first section of this guide will tell you what to look for—the tracks, the feeding areas (browse), droppings (scat), and other signs. For easy reference, you will also find spotter's guides, which combine all of the illustrations of tracks, browse, and scat. Descriptions of the animals follow. They are grouped by the tracks the animal leaves—hoofed, padded, and bird—and each includes a brief description and life-size drawing of its average track. Included at the end of each section are notes about other species that have not been illustrated.

In preparing this guide we have learned that the experience of each person familiar with the woods results in a variety of impressions of what any given animal's tracks look like. We have made every effort to produce a field guide that is as accurate as possible, taking into account this variety of experience. We hope that you will find it useful.

Tracks

When walking in the forest keep in mind that, however deserted it may seem, you are not alone. From the uppermost tree branches to at least a foot under the ground, creatures large and small live out their life cycles. Each of these creatures has left a particular trace. This book will help you learn to read these signatures.

Look, listen—even use your sense of smell. Once an odour has been associated with a particular animal it will never be forgotten, although it may be difficult to describe it to someone else. Watch for animal tracks where wildlife have fed, and learn to recognize the scat or droppings of the various animals.

Tracks of all types can be found in soft mud and snow. The tracks of frogs and toads are left on the soft mud around ponds and mud puddles. Woodcock leave small holes and tracks while probing in the moist soil with their long bills looking for earthworms.

When experience is gained, tracks, even if only tœ nail marks, may also be seen in hard ground. All the tracks illustrated in this book are lifesize. Some have been drawn with dark and shaded area–the darkest portions show the features most commonly seen; the lightest portions show features seen only under ideal conditions. The drawings illustrate the track size of an average adult animal at a walking gait. A change of gait (running) or change of terrain (mud, deep snow) would result in a change in the track recorded.

Foot Forms

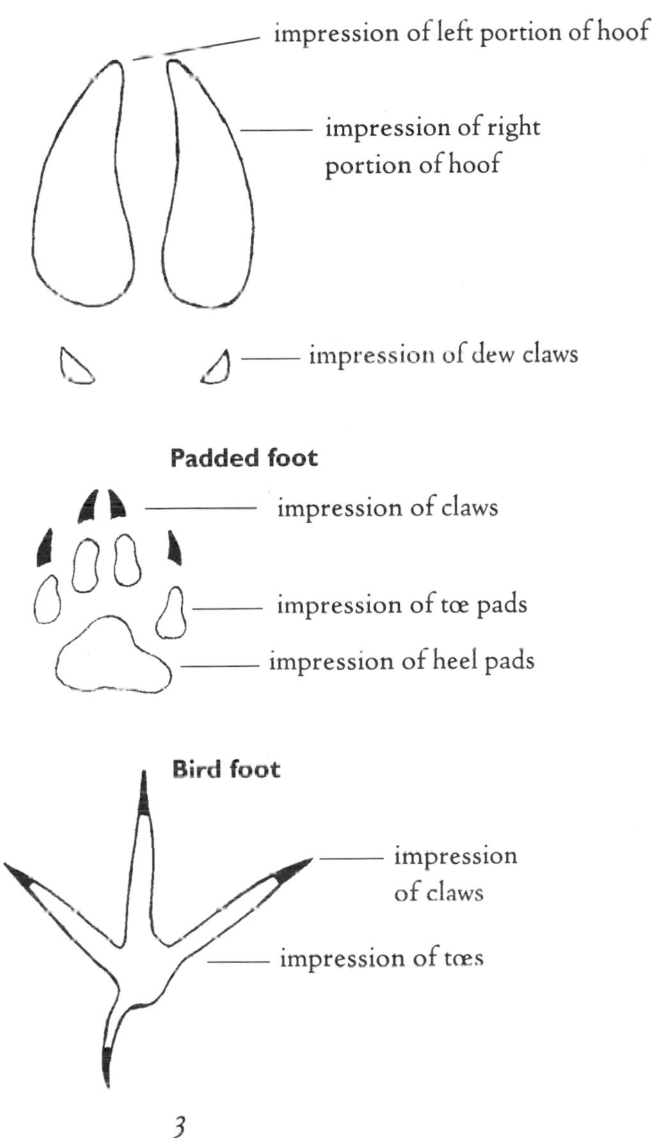
Cloven hoof
impression of left portion of hoof
impression of right portion of hoof
impression of dew claws
Padded foot
impression of claws
impression of tœ pads
impression of heel pads
Bird foot
impression of claws
impression of tœs

Differences in Padded Feet

Certain animals with padded feet, such as members of the cat and dog families, display certain characteristics that will help you to make decisions as to which creature's tracks you are studying

Bobcat

Tœ nails *not* showing. Foot round and heavily furred. Foot pads large, and well defined in track.

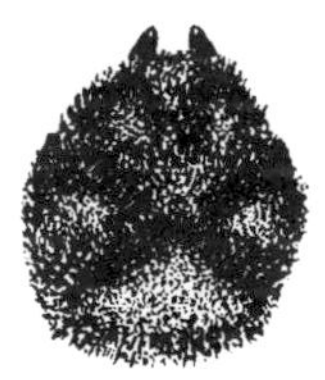

Dog

Tœ nails showing. Foot more pointed than that of cats. Foot pads large.

Red Fox

Tœ nails showing. Foot oval or egg shaped, pointed at front. Heel pad "T" shaped and well defined in track.

Dog and fox tracks will show the typical tœ nails. The heel pad of the fox separates its track from the rest of the dog family. This heel pad on the foot of a fox is in the shape of a "T" bar. The fox track is also more slender, oval or pointed in front.

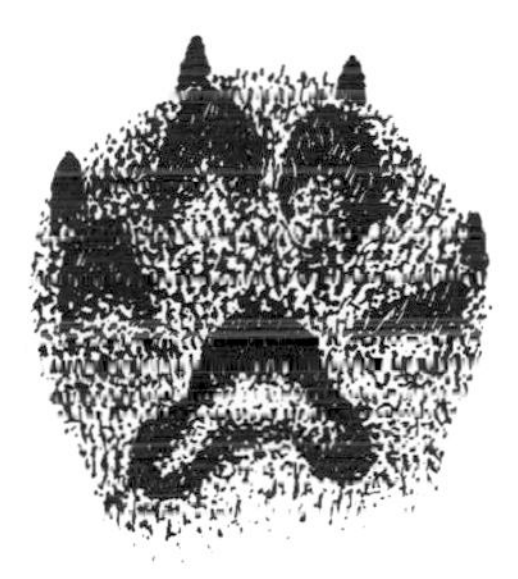

Coyote

Tœ nails showing, foot pads large. Heel pad shaped differently than dog. Heel pad has lobes on each side, extending to the rear

Spotter's Guide to Tracks

Cloven hoofs

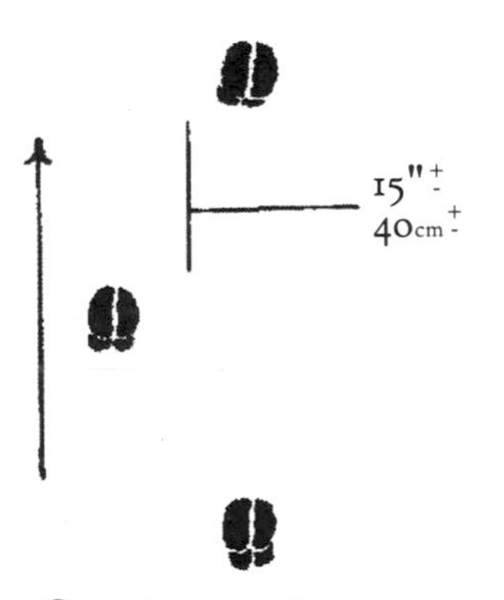

Cow *(see page 20)*

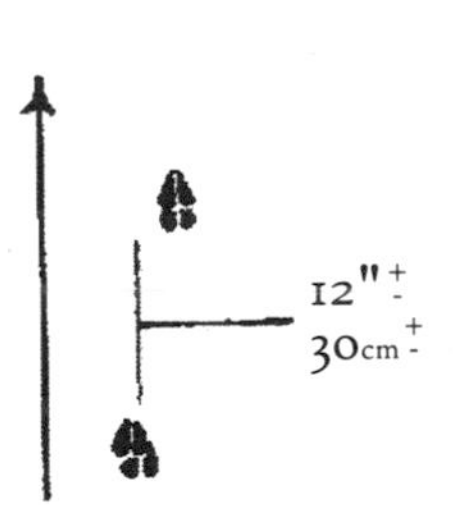

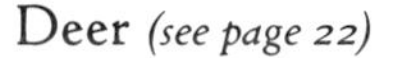

Deer *(see page 22)*

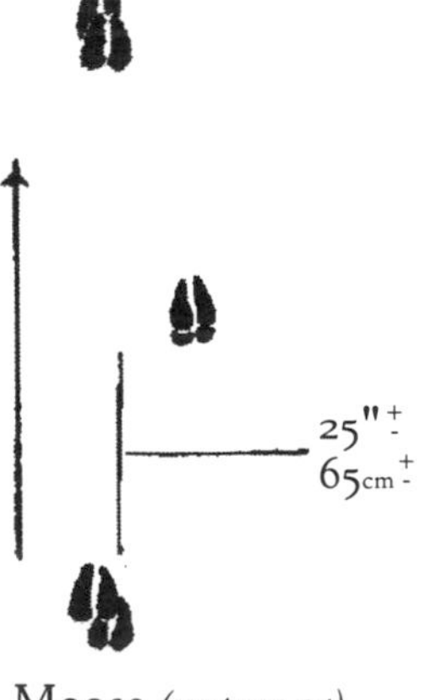

Moose *(see page 24)*

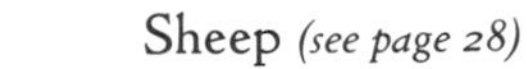

Sheep *(see page 28)*

Padded Feet

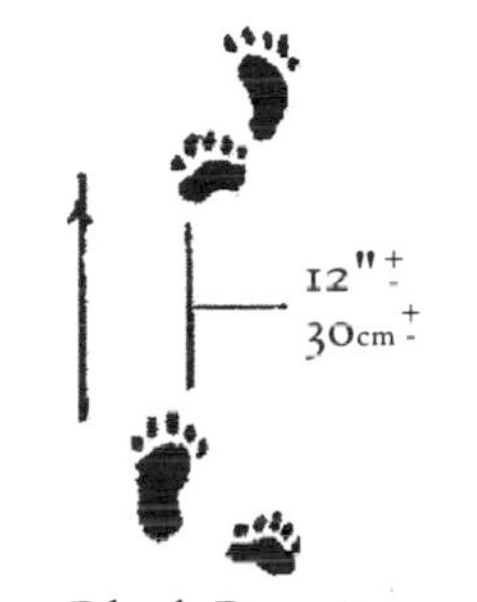

Black Bear *(see page 30)*

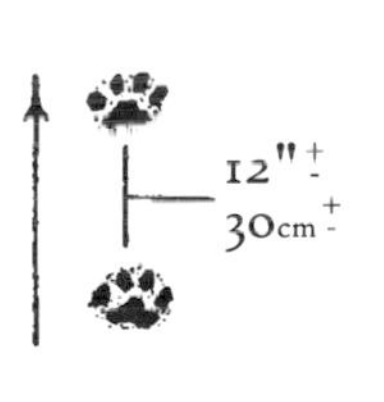

Bobcat *(see page 34)*

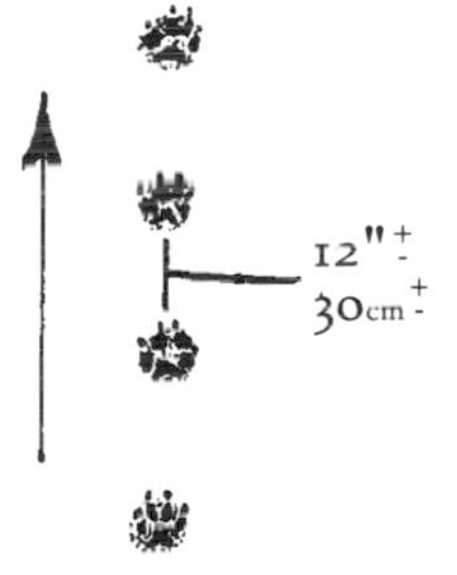

Coyote *(see page 36)*

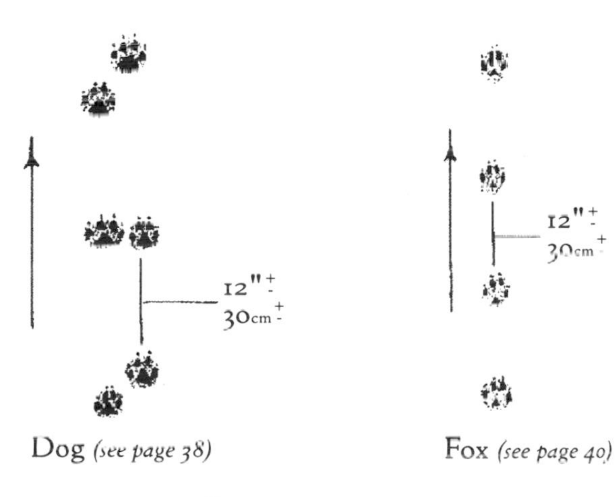

Dog *(see page 38)*

Fox *(see page 40)*

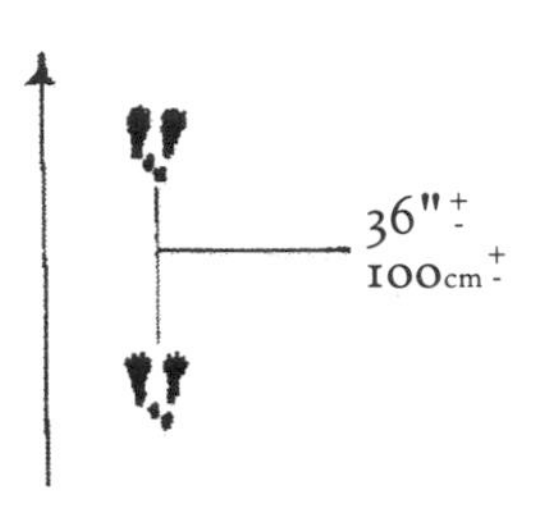

Hare *(see page 42)*

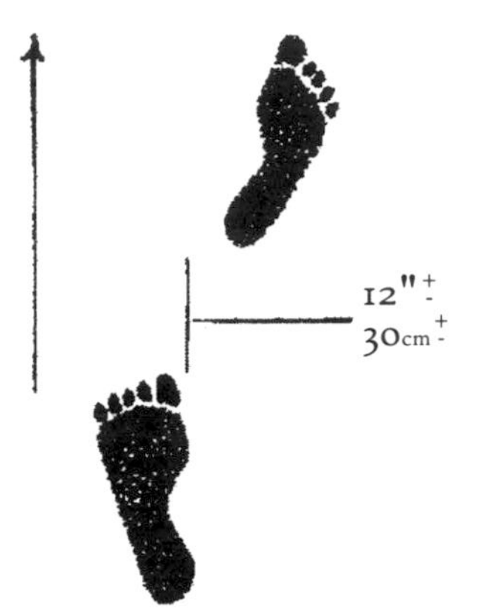

Human *(see page 44)*

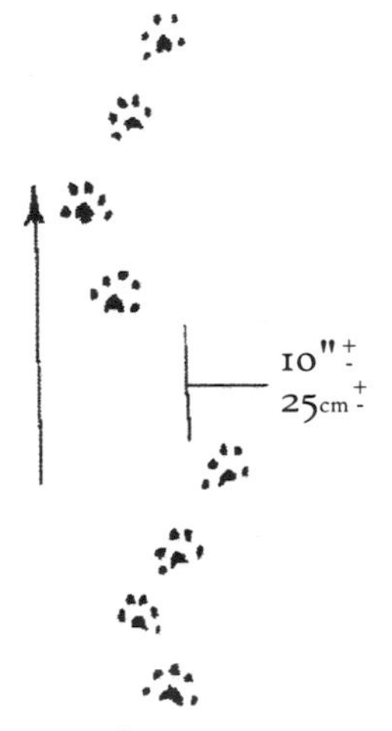

Mink *(see page 46)*

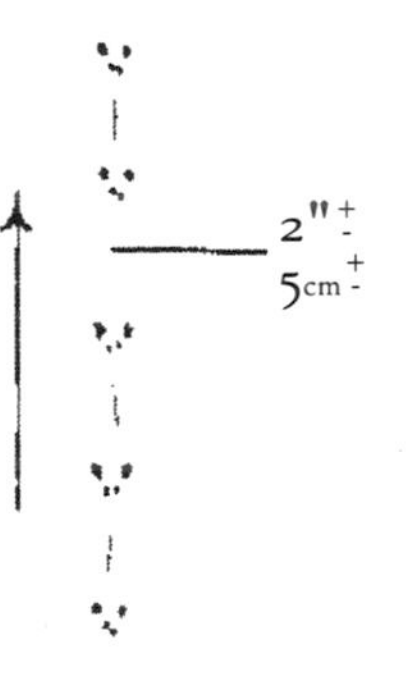

Mouse, White-footed *(see page 48)*

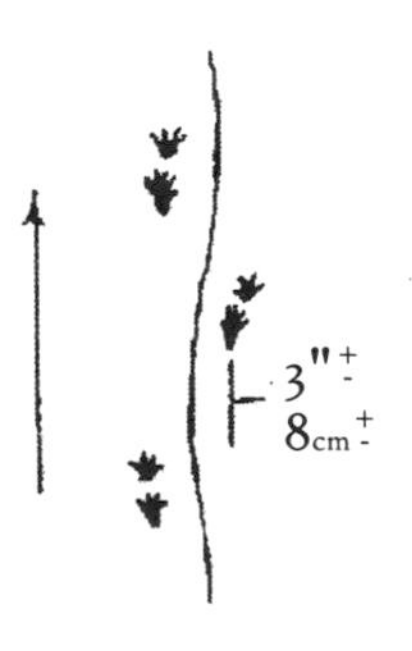

Muskrat *(see page 50)*

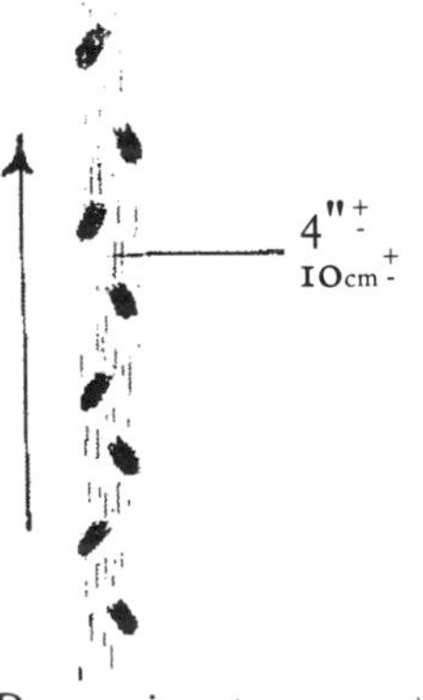

Porcupine *(see page 52)*

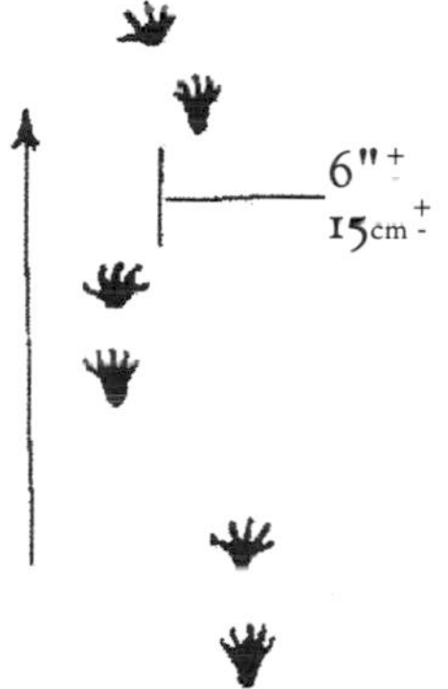

Raccoon *(see page 54)*

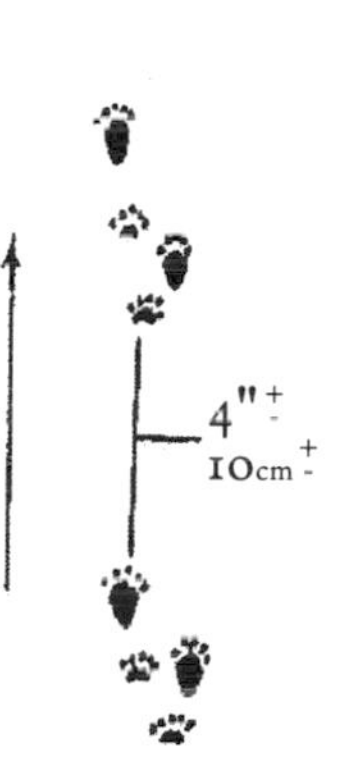

Skunk *(see page 56)*

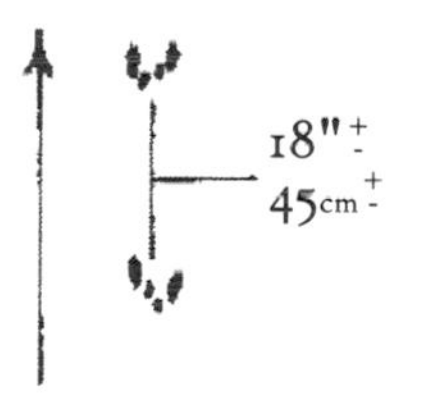

Squirrel *(see page 58)*

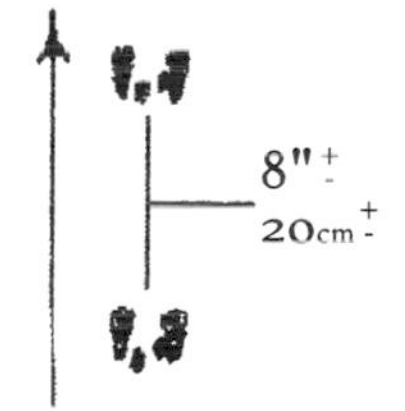

Weasel *(see page 60)*

Bird Tracks

2"±
5cm±

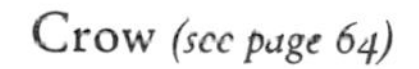
Crow *(see page 64)*

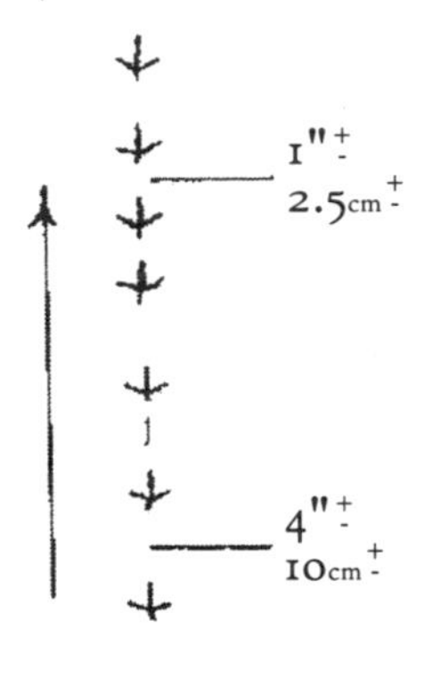

Grouse *(see page 66)*

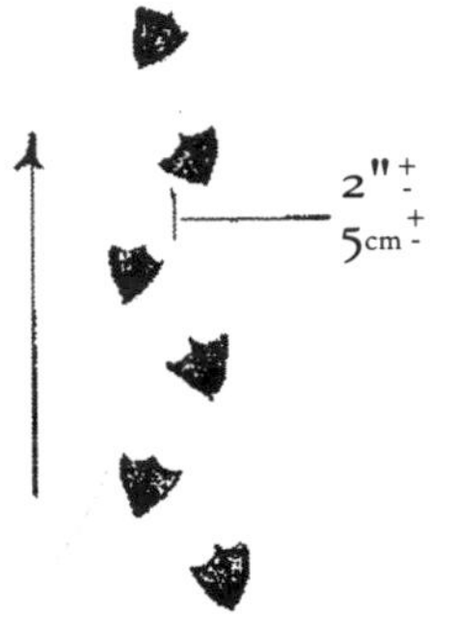

Gull *(see page 68)*

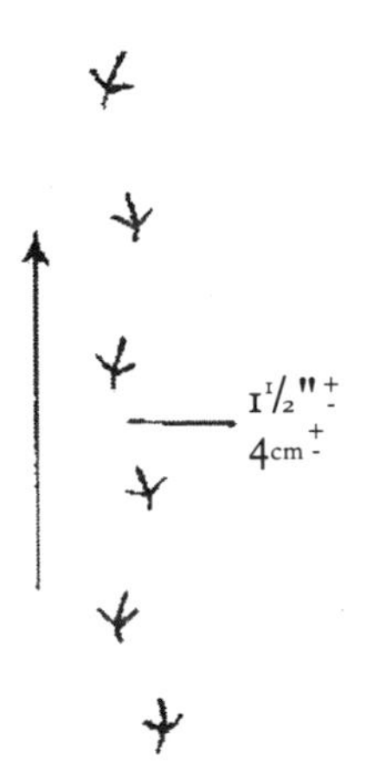

Pigeon *(see page 69)*

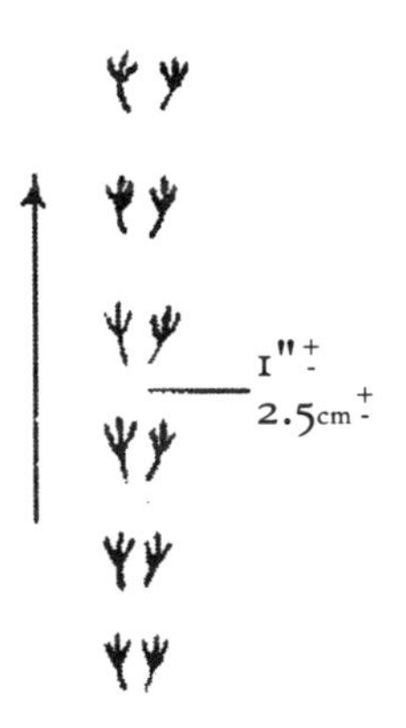

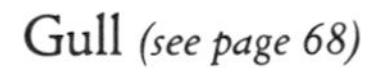

Sparrow *(see page 70)*

Browse

The way an animal bites its food, the way that it disposes of inedible portions, or signs of foraging are browse clues. For example, the presence of black bears can be seen where they have rolled away large stones, dug up ant hills, or torn apart old stumps in search of insects. The remains of a kill covered in leaves means that a wildcat is in the area.

The height above ground level where such browse signs as gnawed-off branches or bark are located can also help identify which animal has eaten there. Remember, however, that a heavy snowfall would increase the height to which an otherwise short hare might reach! Check all the signs (scat, etc.) before reaching a decision.

Spotter's Guide to Browse

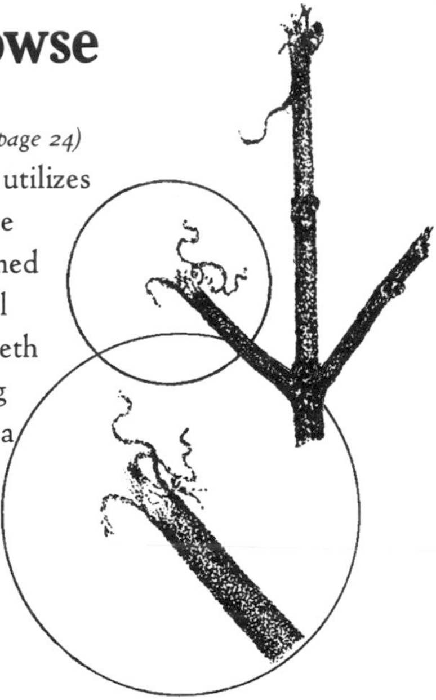

Moose *(see page 24)*

The moose utilizes the tongue, the teeth in the lower jaw, and the toughened upper lip to gnaw off small branches for food. The teeth cut through the twig using the hardened upper lip as a cutting surface. The tongue wraps around the twig as a part of the same action and yanks as the teeth cut. This cutting and tearing action results in many tendrils of bark on the remaining twig.

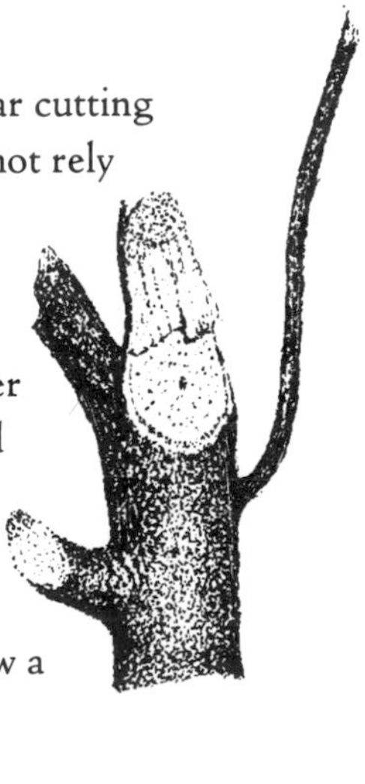

Deer *(see page 22)*

The deer uses a similar cutting action to that of the moose. It dœs not rely upon the tongue to tear the twig, however, but rather only to hold it. The twig stump that remains from deer browse has a smoothly cut lower surface with a slightly wedge-shaped portion protruding from the top.

Small twigs or maple sucker growth are favourite deer browse in winter. These twigs will usually show a rough end where the deer has fed.

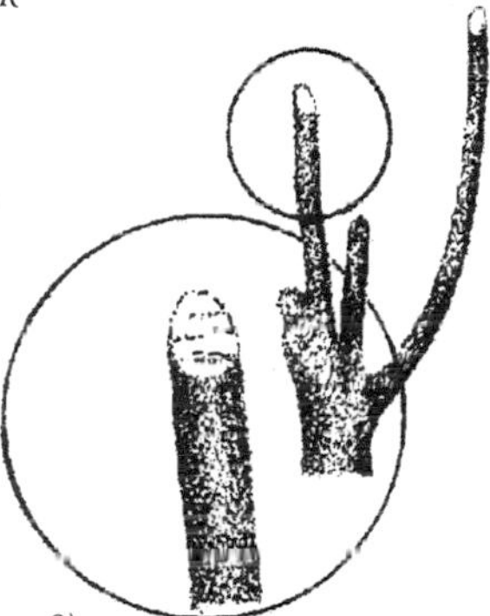

Hare *(see also page 42)*

The hare uses sharp upper and lower teeth like a chisel. The remaining twig stump is fairly smooth, especially when compared to that left by a moose or deer.

Squirrels *(see also page 58)*

Squirrels will strip the winged seeds from the cones of coniferous trees, eat the seeds, and leave the wings behind. The remaining pile is known as a squirrel midden.

Mice *(see also page 48)*

Mice eat the seeds produced by coniferous trees. Unlike the squirrels with their middens, mice scatter the remains. Mice also eat other seeds and nuts.

Grouse *(see also page 66)*

Spruce grouse feed on the buds and needles of spruce and fir. Large quantities of droppings under these trees indicate where they have fed.

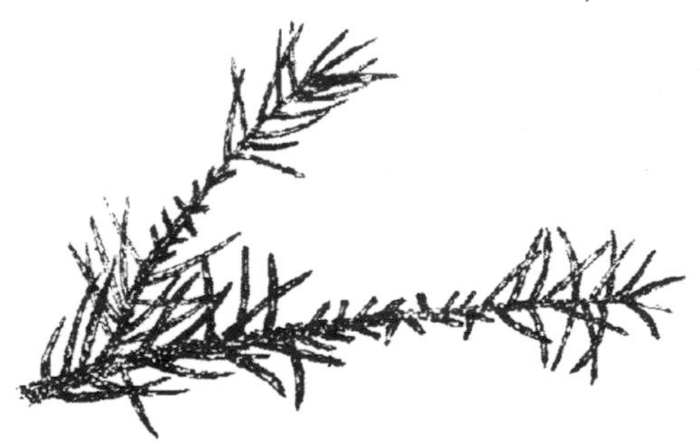

Ruffed grouse *(see also page 66)*

Ruffed grouse prefer hardwood buds and various berries.

Scat

Where animals have fed and what they eat may be discovered by studying animal scat. The appearance of the scat and its location may also be clues to identifying the species. Some birds regurgitate the indigestible parts of their prey. These pellets can sometimes be mistaken for scat (*see p. 71*).

The appearance of scat may vary according to season. Moose and deer droppings during the summer months are soft and formless compared to those found during the winter months. This is due to the large quantity of green food eaten in the summer months; during the winter, woody, fibrous food is eaten.

Spotter's Guide to Scat

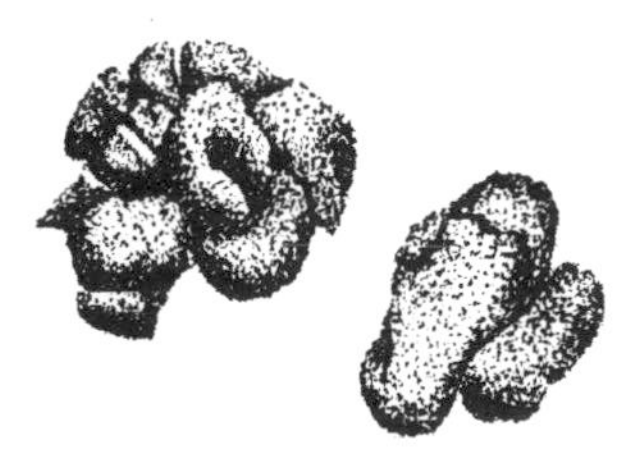

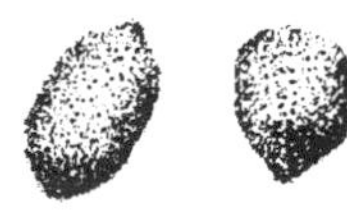

Deer *(see also page 22)*

Summer

Winter

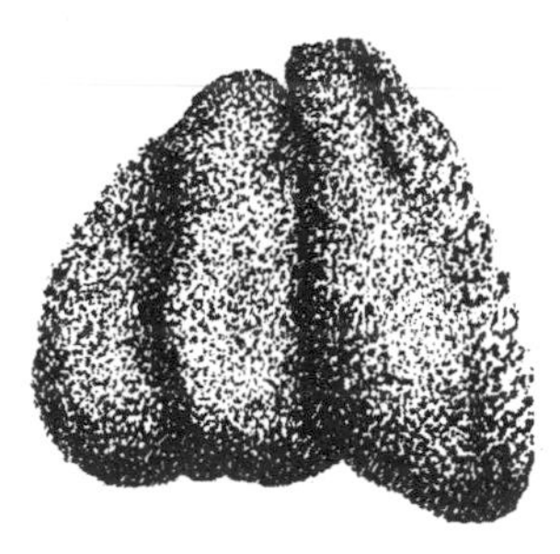

Moose *(see also page 24)*

Summer

Winter

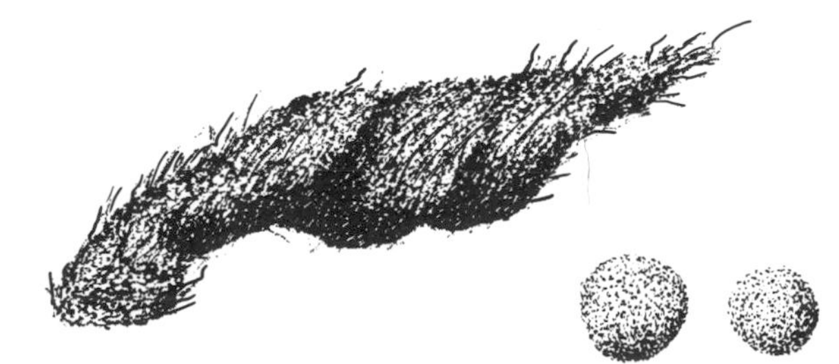

Fox *(see also page 40)*

Hare *(see also page 42)*

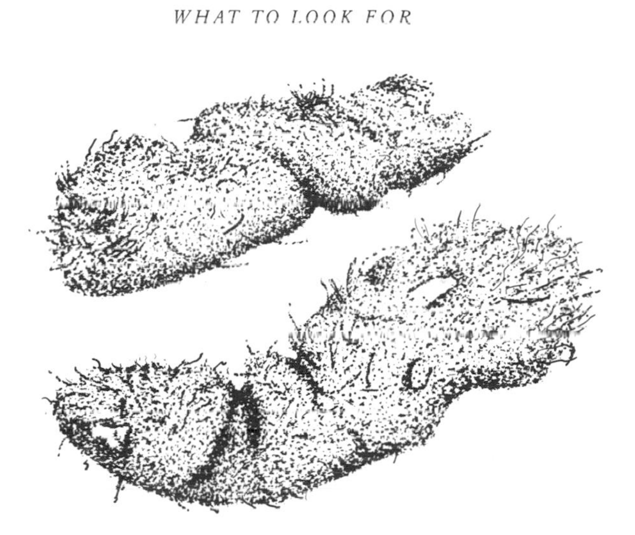

Bobcat *(see also page 34)*

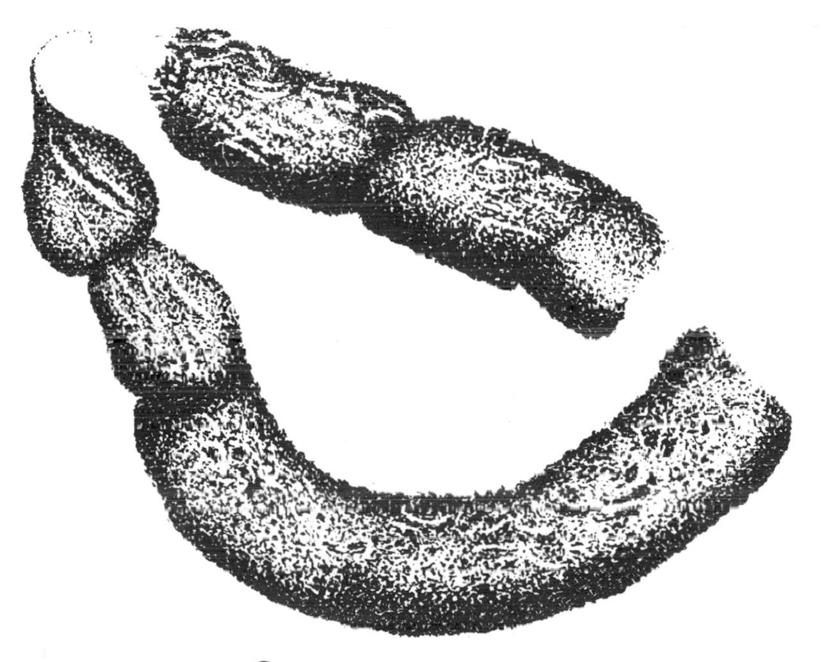

Coyote *(see also page 36)*

Mink *(see also page 46)*

Mouse *(see also page 48)*

Muskrat *(see also page 50)*

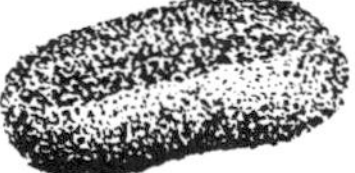

Porcupine *(see also page 52)*

Squirrel *(see also page 58)*

Grouse *(see also page 66)*

Sparrow *(see also page 70)*

Other Signs

Look all around you. Hairs stuck to a tree where an animal has passed may help to identify the size and species concerned. Look for hair on barbed wire fencing as well. Moose and deer polish the velvet or protective skin off their new antlers in September. This would be indicated by the bark and branches being scraped off (generally) young trees, mostly hardwood, two or three feet above the ground. Grooves will often be scraped into the wood of the tree from the antler tines. The bark of the tree will usually be shredded and hanging. Deer and moose antlers fall off during January and February. These cast-off antlers will be fed upon by rodents for the calcium they contain.

Bedding areas may be seen as depressions in the grass or undergrowth. The number and size of these depressions are clues to family groups having lain there.

Remember to listen carefully—for sounds of the animal itself or for activity from other animals. Listen for the characteristic snort of a deer or the whimpering nasal grunt of a porcupine. Study bird books to learn how to distinguish the various bird calls. And use your sense of smell. Of course the lingering odour of a skunk's presence is unmistakable, but other animals also leave odours that are clues to their presence.

Cow

Size and Colour
Varies in colour and size.

Habitat
Domestic.

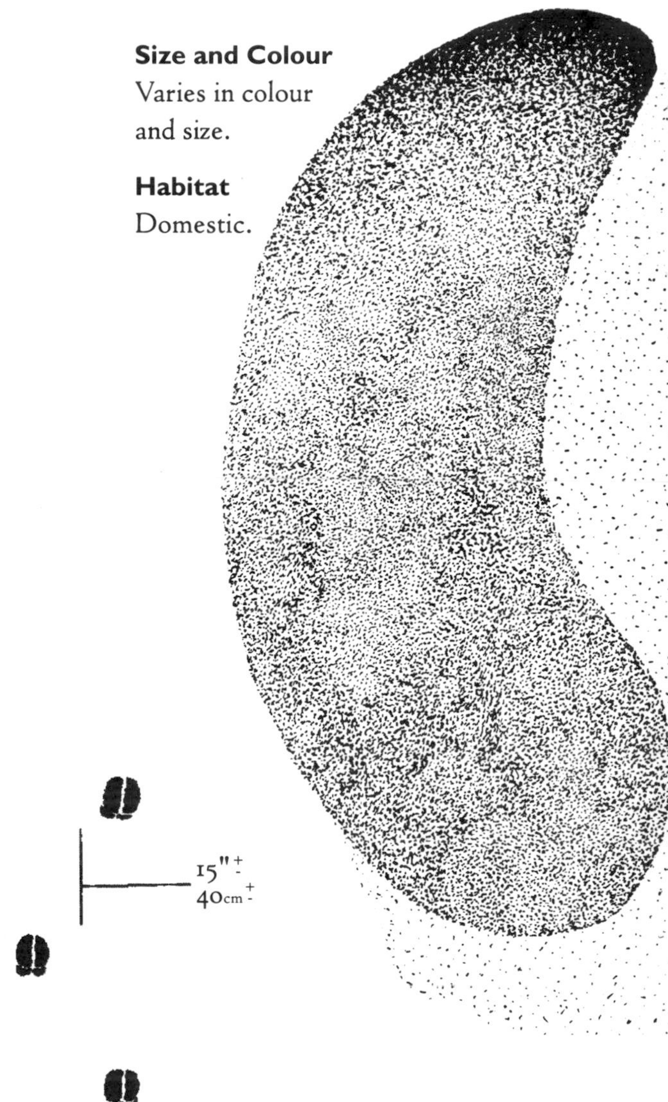

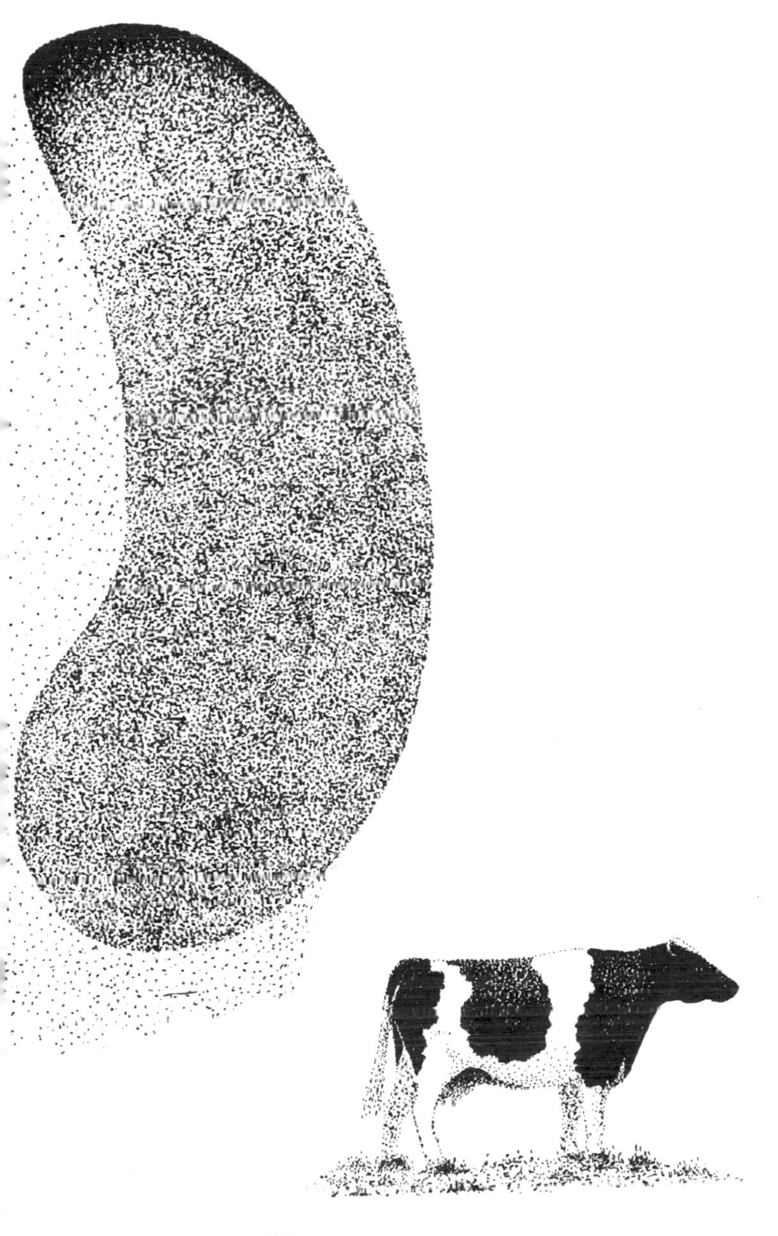

Deer

Size

Height: 0.9–1.1 m (3– 3½ ft)
Weight: ♂ up to 180 kg (400 lbs.)
♀ up to 90 kg (200 lbs.)

Colour

Reddish brown in summer and greyish to greyish brown in winter. Belly, throat, and inside of upper legs whitish. Tail large, bushy, and white underneath.

Habitat

Forests, swamps, and open bush areas nearby.

Notes

By listening and watching the movements of squirrels and blue jays, you can often spot deer before they realize you are present. A white-tail deer wishing to warn other deer in the area of danger runs off with its white tail held erect over its back. When startled, a deer will often blow heavily through its nostrils making a snorting sound.

It is common to find bedding areas of white-tail deer in hayfields and dry bogs. Usually this is a depression in the grass about 90 cm (3 ft.) long by 45 cm (18 in.) wide. If made by a dœ and a fawn, there will be the large bed of the dœ with the small depression of the fawn within a few feet.

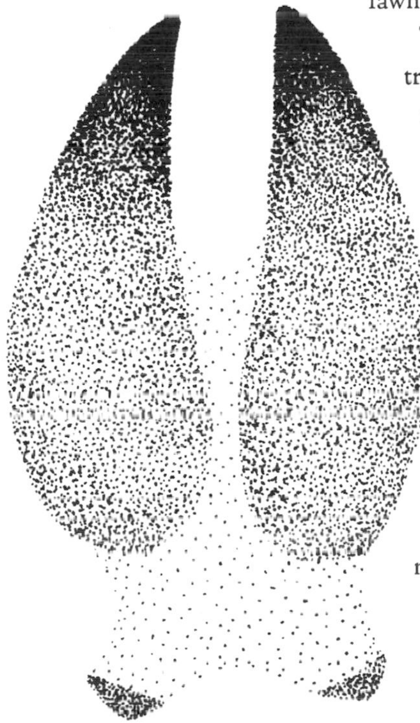

Trees that lean over the trail often have hair stuck to the bark or branches. If the hair is grey with white and less than 1.2 m (4 ft.) above ground, it will probably be from white-tail deer. Barbed wire fencing is also a good place to look for hair. With just an inch (2.5cm) of snow on the ground, a buck deer will show drag marks. This is caused by the buck not lifting its feet as high as a dœ.

Moose

Size

Height: 1.5–2 m (5–6½ ft.)
Weight: ♂ up to 635 kg (1400 lbs.)
♀ up to 360 kg (800 lbs.)

Colour

Upper parts blackish brown to black; belly and lower legs brownish grey; muzzle grey.

Habitat

Forests with lakes and swamps.

Notes

Large beds in swamps and bogs, 1.2 or 1.5 m (4 or 5 ft.) long and 60–90 cm (2–3 ft.) wide, indicate where moose have lain. A large bed with a medium and small depression nearby indicate that a bull, cow and calf moose lay in these spots.

Check trees along the trail for hair. If the hair is black with a few white hairs and more than 1.2 m (4 ft.) above the ground, it is probably from a moose. Like deer, moose leave characteristic marks where they polish their new antlers on hardwood branches.

Moose

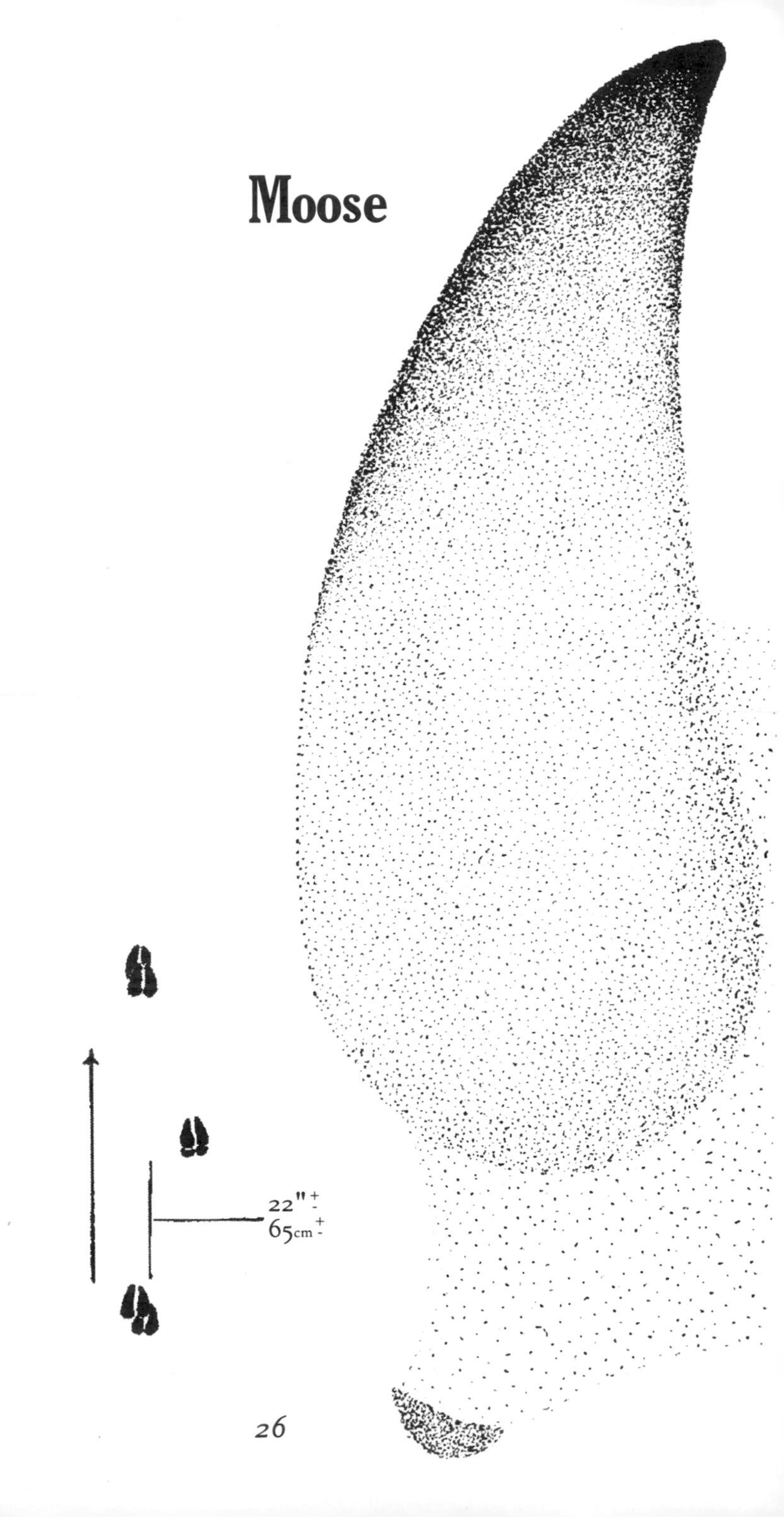

Sheep

Size

Varies in size.

Colour

White or black or brown or grey or combination of two of the above.

Habitat

Domestic.

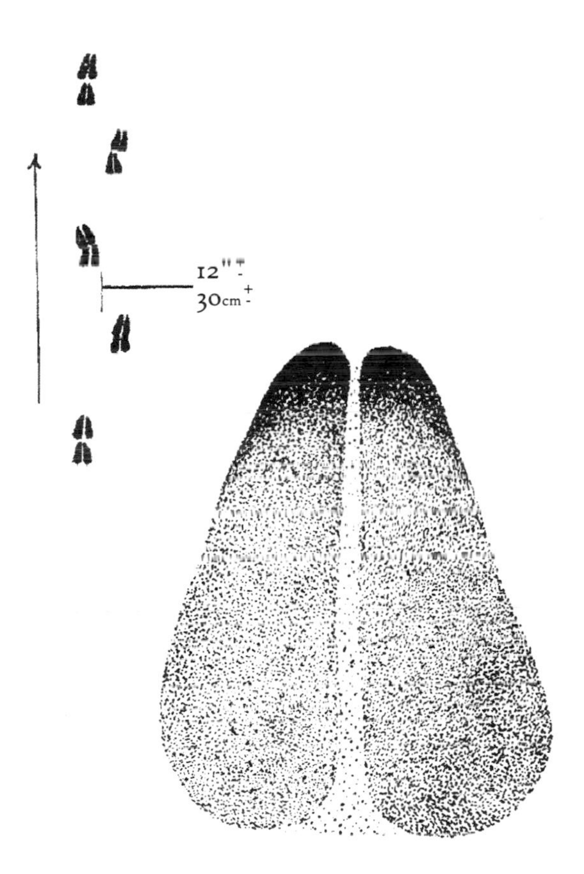
12" ±
30cm ±

Black Bear

Size

Length: head & body 1.5–1.8 m (5–6 ft.)
Weight: up to 215 kg (470 lbs.)

Colour

Black, blackish rusty, or dark brown to pale cinnamon. Muzzle brownish. Large white spot on chest.

Habitat

Mixture of forest and open country

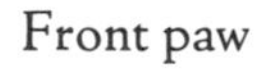

Front paw

Notes

The black bear track in snow or mud will show an impression of the entire foot with the points of greatest pressure being the most distinctive. The heel pad and track of the rear foot is larger than that of the front foot. The bear walks in a pigeon-tœd manner.

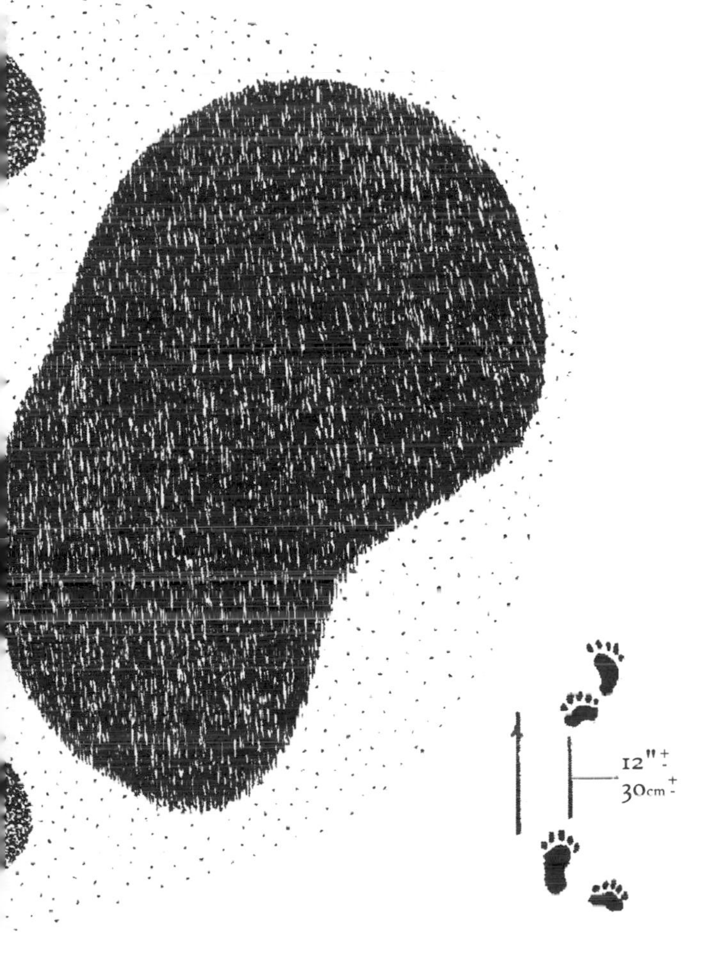

12" ±
30cm ±

The black bear will roll large stones, dig up ant hills, or tear old stumps apart to get at ants and insects. The bear also eats berries in summer and raids apple orchards in the fall. Due to the number of apples eaten, bear scat in the fall will usually resemble a pile of apple sauce dumped on the ground. Evidence of bears having clawed and broken branches from apple trees can be seen in some areas.

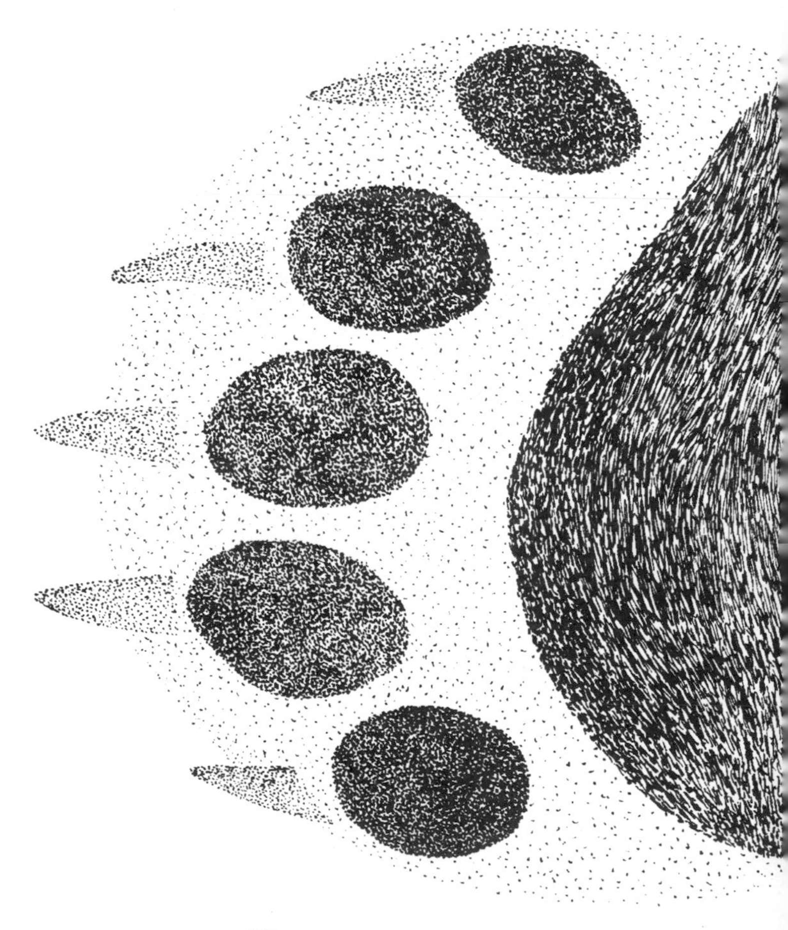

Rear paw

Bobcat

Size

Length: head & body 55–75 cm (25"–30")
Weight: up to kg (40 lbs.)

Colour

Upper parts pale yellowish brown to reddish brown mixed with grey and brownish or black becoming whitish spotted with white on the underparts; underside of tail white.

Habitat

Swamps and forests.

Notes

Cat tracks, be they domestic or wild, show only the mark of the pads, not the claws. A wandering line of prints through the forest may be made by a Bobcat. The rear foot is almost always placed in the track of the front foot. Each foot track is almost the same distance apart.

Finding remains of a large animal partly covered by leaf litter or branches indicates where a Bobcat fed and covered the remains for a future meal.

Bobcats seem to prefer certain spots to toilet, usually a high spot on a trail or woods road. Several piles of cat scat of different ages can usually be found at one of these toilets. Their scat usually contains large quantities of hair and crushed bone. Snowshoe hare is the Bobcat's chief food source but quite often squirrel and mouse remains can be found.

Coyote

Size

Length: head & body 90–110 cm (36"–44")
Weight: 15–30 kg (30–60 lbs.)

Colour

Upper body brownish grey with some black-tipped hair. A mane of 10–15 cm (4–6 in.) hair, brownish and white with black tipped hair running down the neck and along the backbone to the base of the tail. Some white under chin. Reddish fawn legs with a black line down shin bone.

Tail heavily furred with a black spot halfway down its length.

Habitat

Mixture of forest and open country.

Notes

The first coyote was taken in Nova Scotia near Country Harbour, Guysborough County on February 1, 1977. Coyotes are now found throughout Nova Scotia both on the mainland and on Cape Breton Island.

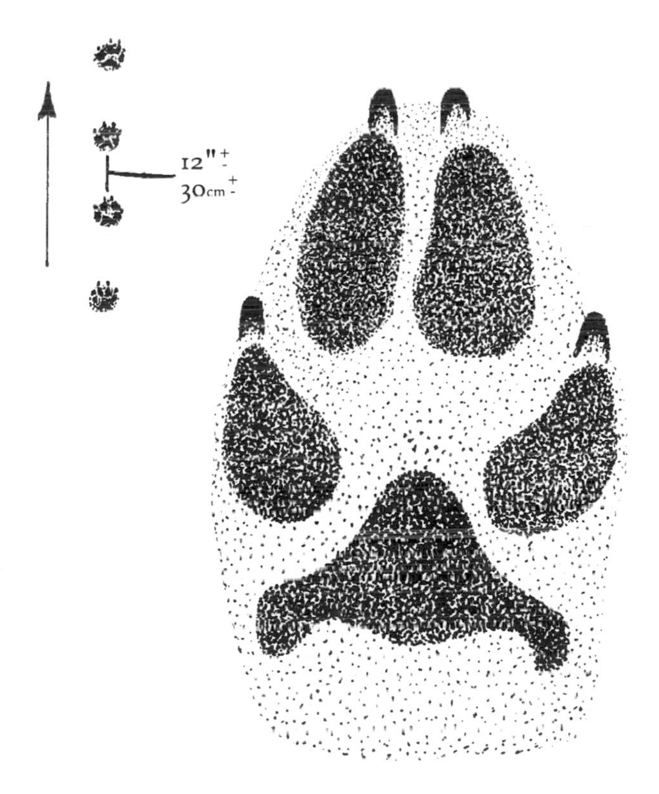

Dog

Size

Varies greatly with the wide variety of domestic species available and therefore impossible to generalize.

Colour

Varies according to species.

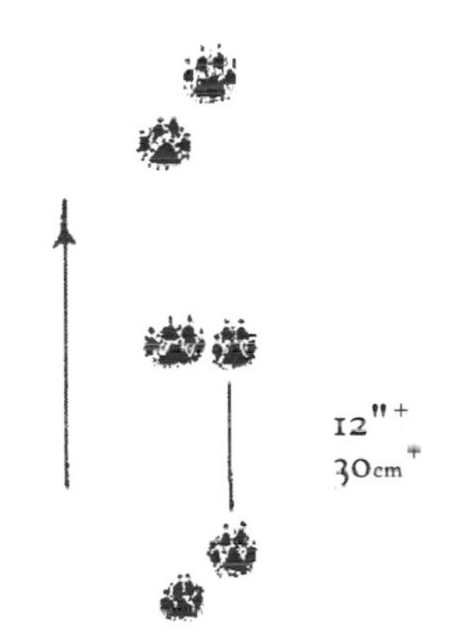
12"+
30cm+

Fox

Size

Length: head & body 55–65 cm (22"–25")
Weight: up to 6.7 kg (15 lbs.)

Colour

Rich golden reddish yellow with black feet and legs. Chest, underparts and tip of tail white. Fur long, full and very soft.

Habitat

Mixture of forest and open country preferred.

Notes

The red fox builds its den under buildings, in natural caverns in the woods, and in holes dug by the mother. Its bark is a quick, high-pitched sound similar to that of a dog. A fox feeds on meat, carrion, plants, and berries. Some foxes have become city dwellers because of the easy access to garbage and highway litter.

Fox give off a strong odour when startled.

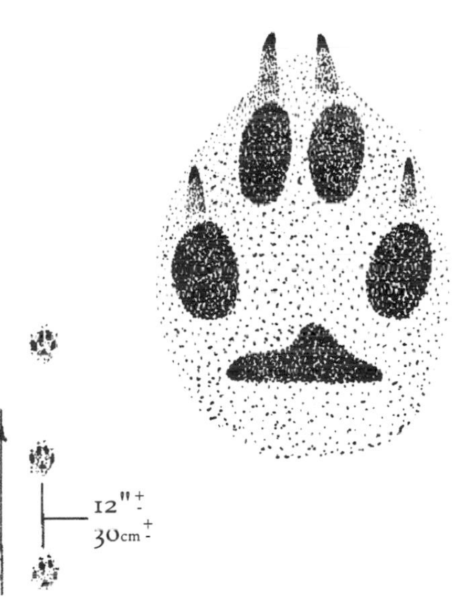

Snowshoe Hare

Size

Length: head & body 33–45 cm (13"–18")
Weight: up to 1.8 kg (4 lbs.)

Colour

White in winter, dark brown in summer.

Habitat

Swamps, forests, thickets.

Notes

This large-footed hare spreads its toes to increase its foot area, allowing it to travel over snow with ease. The snowshoe hare uses its front feet to dig for tender sprouts buried under the snow.

The snowshoe hare makes a depression in the ground or the snow where it sits perfectly still when not feeding. These depressions are called the hare's bed or "form," and are usually under low-hanging evergreen boughs. One may see hares sitting in their forms under fence rails and fallen trees. The hare's round, dark eye is usually the first thing you will notice. Hares have been known to make their form 1 m (3 ft.) above the ground in the crotch of a tree.

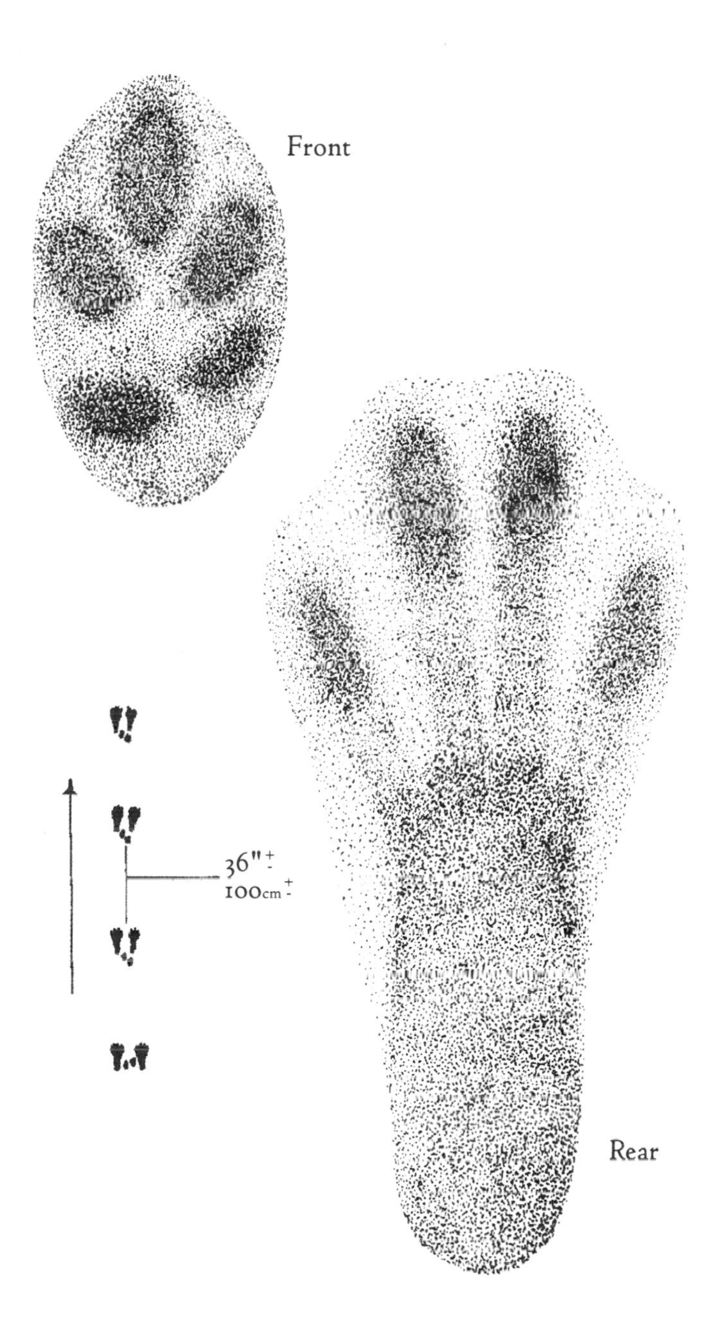
Front
36"±
100cm±
Rear

Human

Habitat

Domestic

Size and Colour

Varies in colour and size.

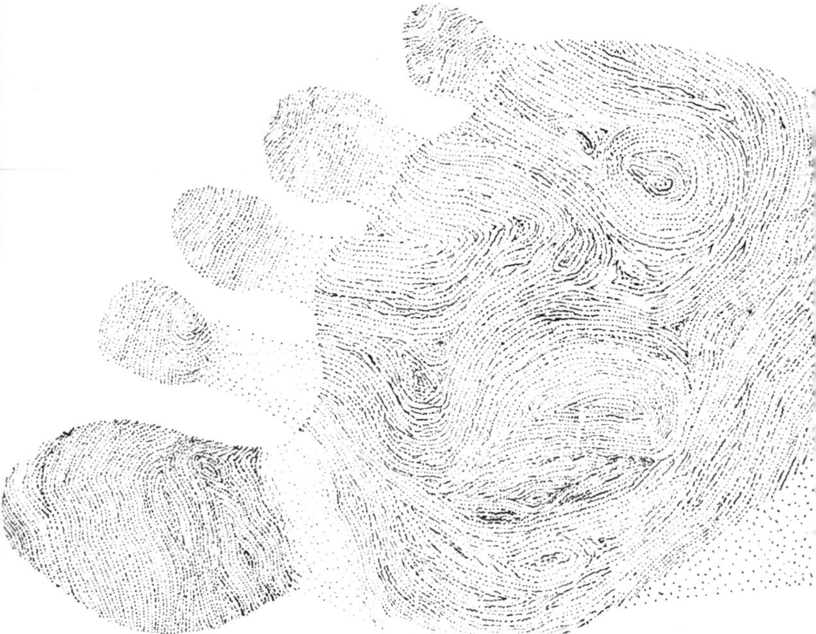

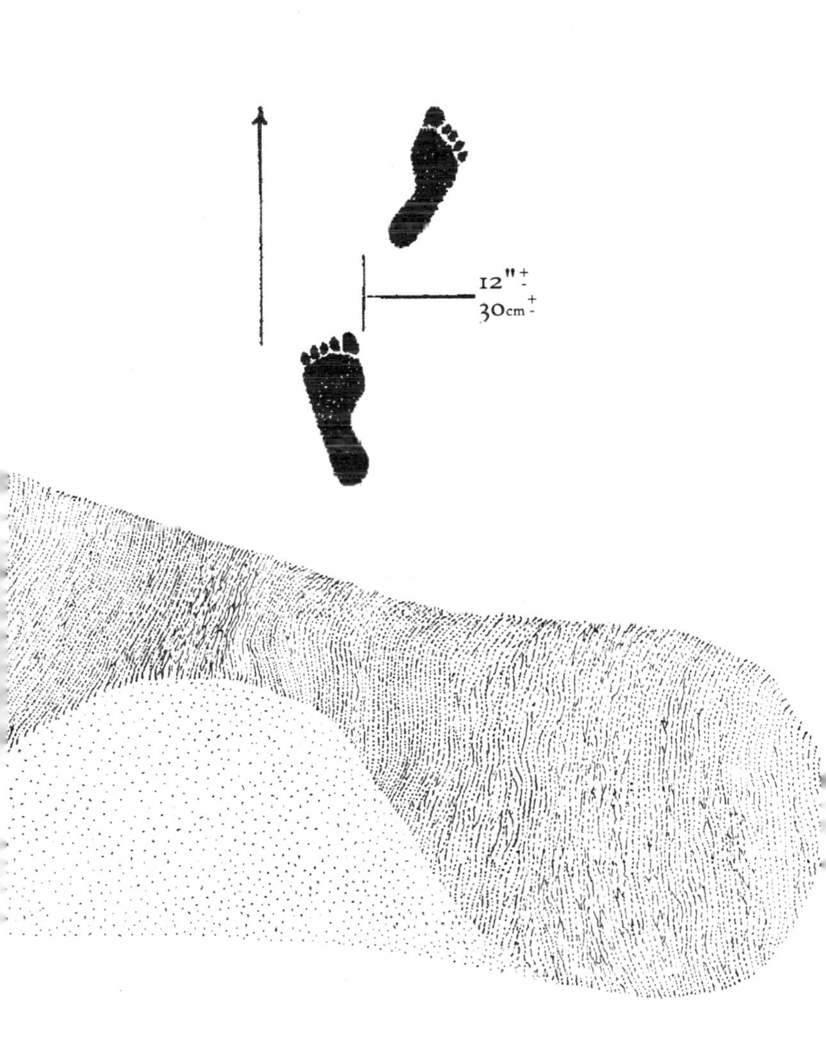
12"±
30cm±

Mink

Size

Length: head & body
♂ 33–43 cm (13"–17")
♀ 30–36 cm (12"–14")
Weight: ♂ up to 1.4 kg (3 lbs.)
♀ up to 1 kg (2 lbs.)

Colour

Usually rich dark brown with a white chin patch. Tail is slightly bushy.

Habitat

Along streams and lakes.

Notes

Mink tracks may be seen leaving open water and leading across frozen water or snow-covered country to the next open water. Mink tracks are similar to squirrel tracks but larger.

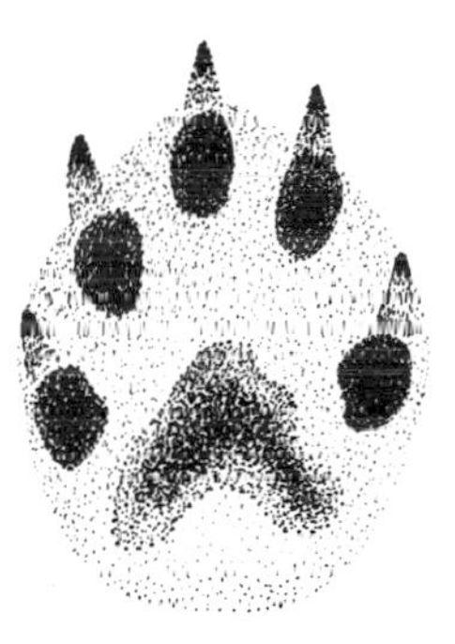

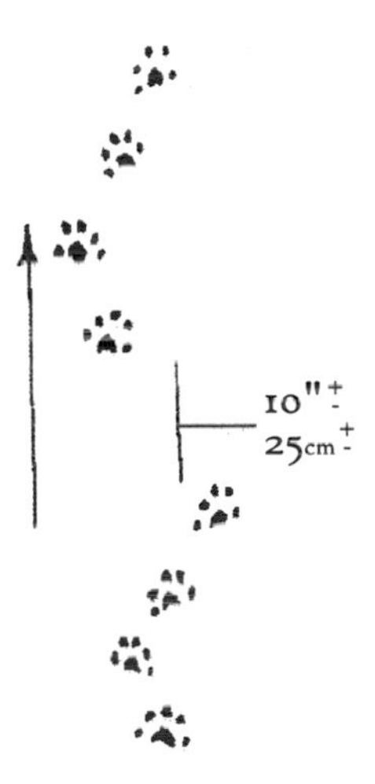

White-footed Mouse

Size

Length: head & body
9–10.6 cm ($3^{3}/_{5}$"–$4^{1}/_{5}$")
Weight: up to 31 g ($1^{1}/_{10}$ oz.)

Colour

Upper parts pale to rich reddish brown; belly and feet white.

Habitat

Wooded or brushy areas preferred; sometimes open areas.

Notes

White-footed mice and Red-backed voles may be found in forested areas, living amid the root systems of hardwood trees. Look for holes, tunnels, or evidence of feeding—empty seed hulls, etc., at the base of trees.

With 2.5 cm (1 in.) of snow on the ground, Meadow vole trails or tunnels are easily visible in fields and clearings. White-footed and deer mice will be the only mice above the snow in the forest during the winter.

Mouse and vole trails can be found in grass and hay fields, especially around the edges close to rose bushes and other cover. Scat may be found on stones or bits of wood.

Mice eat seeds produced by coniferous trees. Unlike squirrels, which leave piles, or middens, mice scatter the remains. Mice also eat other seeds and nuts.

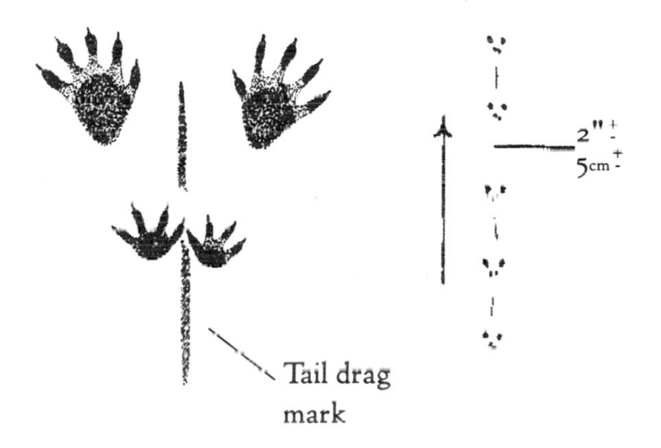

Muskrat

Size

Length: head & body 25–35 cm (10"–14")
Weight: up to 1.8 kg (4 lbs.)

Colour

Rich brown; fur dense, overlaid with coarse guard hairs; tail long, naked, scaly and black; flattened from top to bottom and used as a rudder when swimming.

Habitat

Marshes, edges of ponds, lakes and streams; cat tails, rushes, waterlilies, open water.

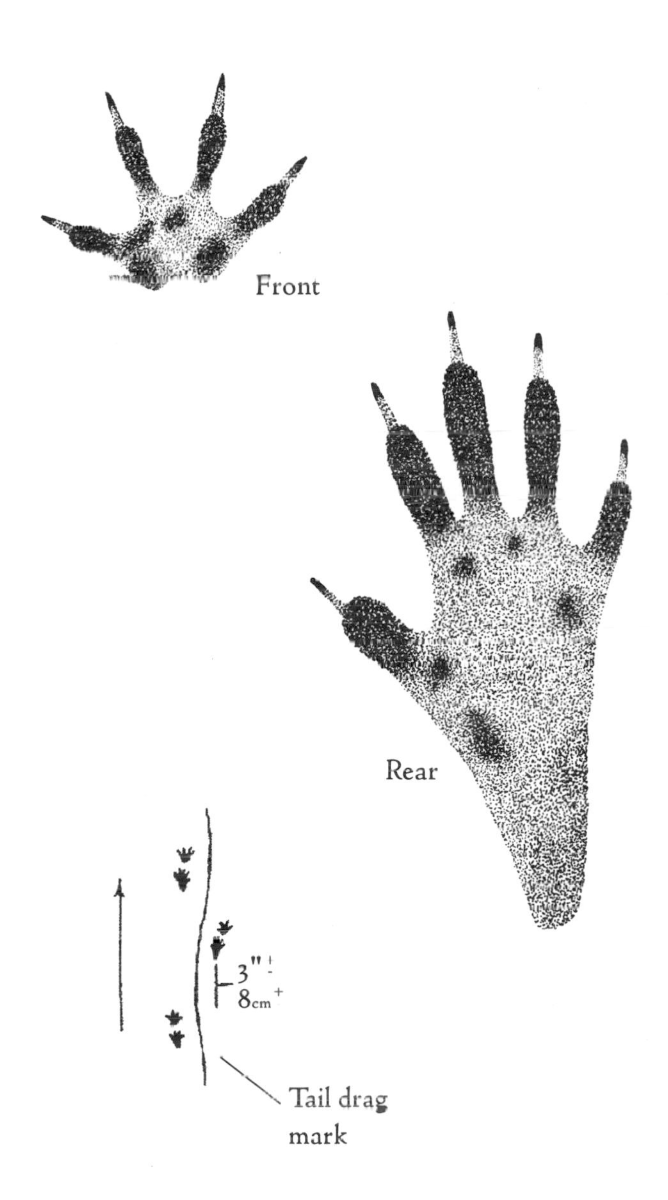
Front
Rear
3"±
8cm±
Tail drag
mark

Porcupine

Size

Length: head & body 45–55 cm (18"–22")
Weight: up to 13.6 kg (30 lbs.)

Colour

Blackish to dark brownish liberally sprinkled with whitish- or yellowish-tipped hairs; spines yellowish white tipped with brown or black.

Front

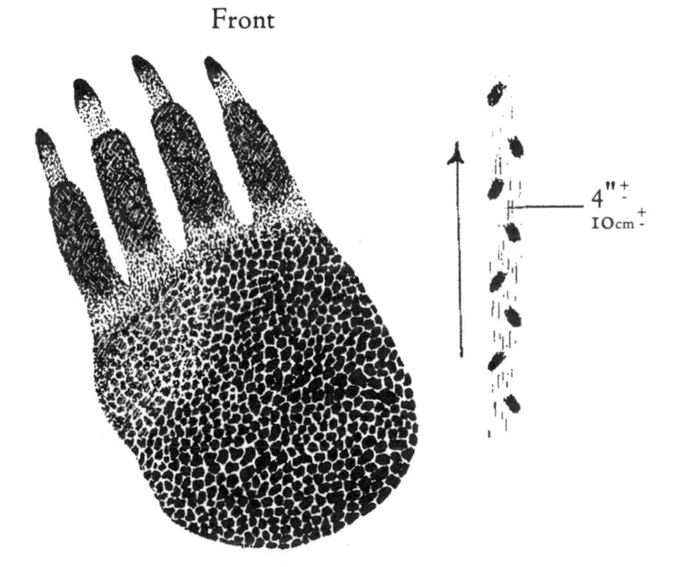

Habitat

Usually forested areas, but occasionally away from trees if brush is available.

Notes

The porcupine, a spiny rodent, feeds on the bark of various trees. Contrary to popular belief it dœs not throw its quills. Its tracks indicate its pigeon-tœd way of walking.

If you hear whimpering nasal grunts (some drawn out for 4 or 5 seconds) it is probably a porcupine calling. They usually call in the evening and during the night, especially in September and October, which is the mating season.

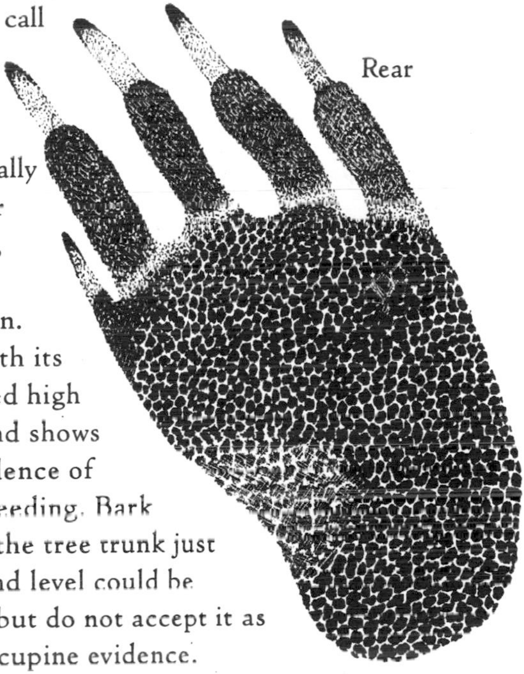

Rear

A tree with its bark stripped high above ground shows definite evidence of porcupine feeding. Bark eaten from the tree trunk just above ground level could be porcupine, but do not accept it as definite porcupine evidence. Snowshoe hares will eat the bark off hardwoods during the winter; mice prefer to eat the bark of young fruit trees. Check the area for scat or tracks before making a decision.

Raccoon

Size

Length: head & body 45–70 cm (18"–28")
Weight: up to 15.8 kg (35 lbs.)

Colour

Pepper and salt mixture. May be recognized by black mask over eyes and alternating rings of yellowish white and black on tail.

Habitat

A forest dweller living throughout the province.

Notes

Raccoon hind feet tracks look like those of miniature, bare human feet. The front feet tracks look like small hand prints. They are similar to hands and are used in the same way.

Raccoons are scavengers that live within city limits as well as in deep forests. They can pry the cover off the best sealed garbage can, open doors, etc. These animals can be vicious if cornered.

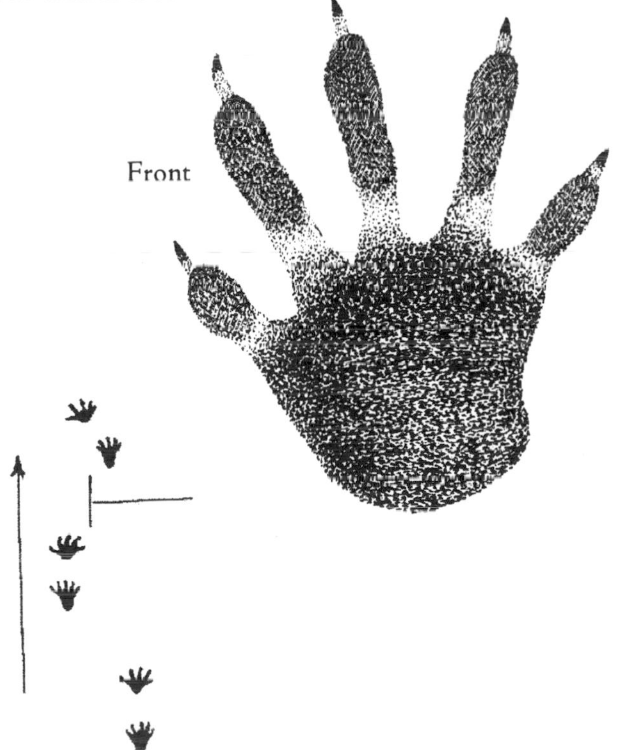

Striped Skunk

Size

Length: head & body 33–45 cm (13"–18")
Weight: up to 6.4 kg (14 lbs.)

Colour

Black body; narrow white stripe up middle of forehead becomes broad at the nape of the neck and divides into two white stripes running down either side of the body.

Habitat

Semi-open country; mixed woods and brushland.

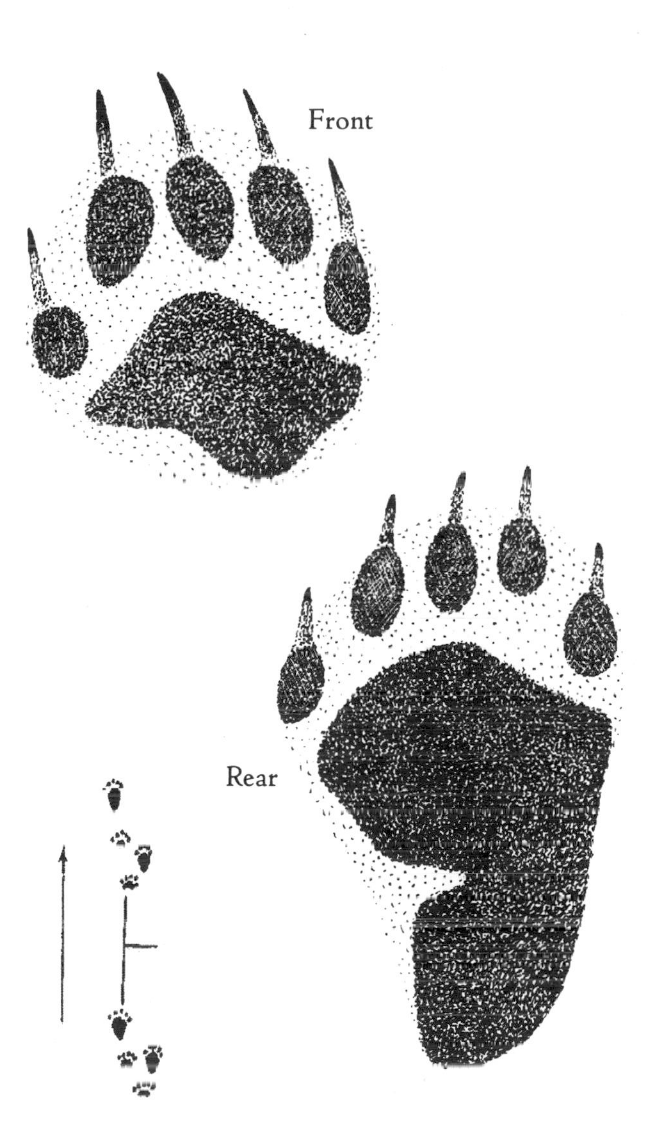
Front
Rear

Red Squirrel

Size

Length: head & body 18–20 cm (7"–8")
Weight: up to 308g (11 oz.)

Colour

Uniformly yellowish or reddish with whitish belly; paler on back in winter; black line along side in summer.

Habitat

Pine and spruce or mixed hardwood forests; swamps

Notes

The track of the red squirrel is like that of a small hare track. As well as eating the seeds of coniferous trees (*see p. 13 for description of a squirrel midden*), squirrels will also eat other seeds, nuts, and berries.

Squirrels call back and forth to keep each other posted. If an intruder enters their territory they chatter vigorously from the trees above.

Flying squirrels nest or rest during daylight in old woodpecker nests, hollow trees, or even in hollow fence posts.

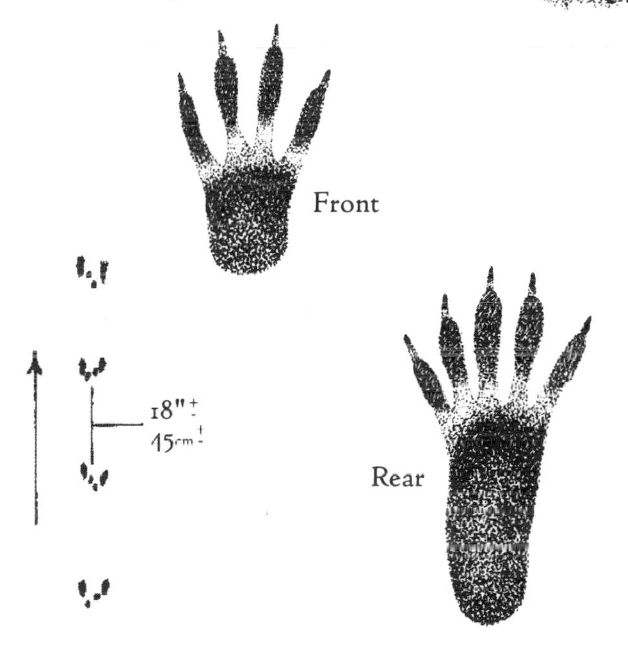

Short tail Weasel (Ermine)

Size

Length: head & body
♂ 15–23 cm (6"–9")
♀ 17–19 cm (5–7½ ")
Weight: ♂ up to 170 g (6 oz.)
♀ up to 85 g (3 oz.)

Colour

Dark brown with white underparts and feet in summer; white in winter. It always has a black tip on the tail.

Habitat

Bushy or wooded areas.

Notes

Members of the weasel family are musk carriers which give off a strong odour. Every animal has its own distinctive odour which can be distinguished with experience.

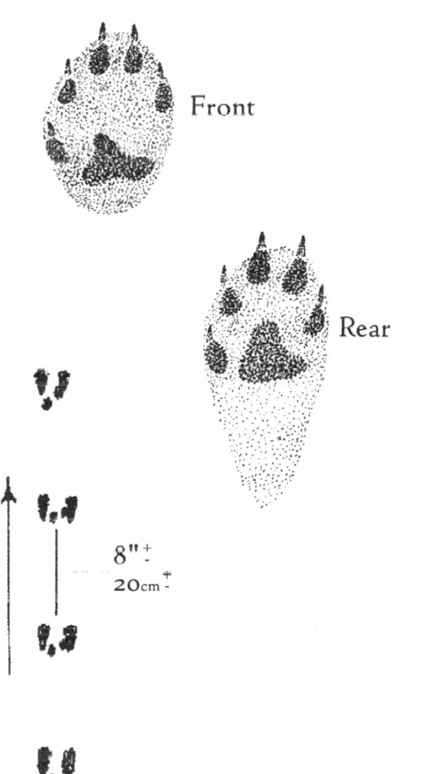

Other Species

Beavers

Beavers do not always build dams. We find "bank beavers" along some of our bigger rivers and in some lakes. These bank beavers tunnel their houses out of the stream or lake shore.

A house that beavers are using will sometimes have no snow around the vent, as the body heat from the beavers below will melt the snow around it.

The beaver builds scent mounds around its pond for territory markers. These mounds are small piles of soil, leaves, and sticks on which the beaver leaves its castor oil scent.

Moles

The presence of the star-nosed mole can be detected by mounds of loose ground in fields and lawns. Moles prefer wet soil. They are weak-eyed and spend most of their lives in tunnels underground, feeding on earthworms and insects. Being a good swimmer this mole also feeds on small fish and aquatic insects.

Otters

Otter tracks in winter may be seen along the edge of frozen waterways. The track shows where the animal has pushed its body along through the snow, using its large webbed rear feet in a sliding motion. Otter tracks may be seen particularly during February and March as they travel along snow-covered stream banks. This is their breeding season.

Frogs

The tracks of frogs and toads are left on the soft mud around ponds and mud puddles.

Crow

Size

38–48cm (15"–17")

Colour

Black

Habitat

Throughout the province

Notes

There can sometimes be confusion of the crow with the raven. Crows are smaller and when they fly their wings move well above a horizontal line above their back. Ravens, when flying, do not raise their wings above the horizontal line. Crows are wing flappers whereas ravens are gliders and may be seen soaring high in the sky.

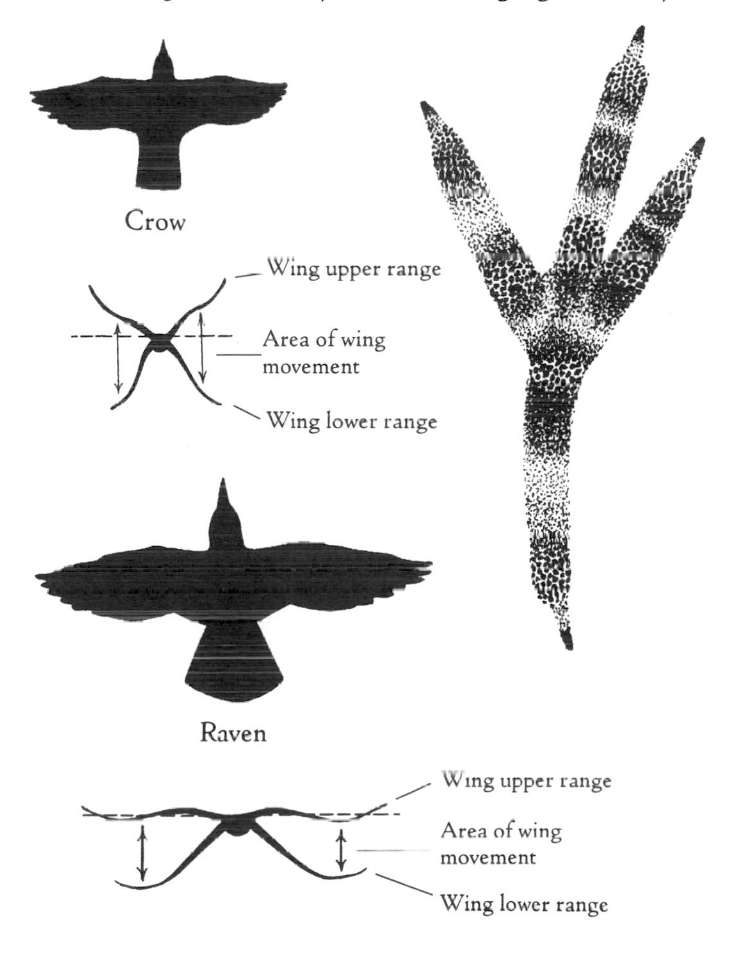

Ruffed Grouse

Size

30.5–35.5cm (12"–14")

Colour

Red brown or grey brown. It has a fan-shaped tail with a broad black band near the end.

Habitat

Brushy woodlands.

Notes

Spruce and ruffed grouse tracks may be seen where the birds have walked about looking for seeds, buds, and berries.

When startled, grouse fly away with a loud flutter of wings. The ruffed grouse makes a louder noise and is more timid than the spruce grouse.

Grouse roost areas may be seen usually in a sheltered spot close to the ground. A small pile of droppings may also be found. Ruffed grouse may also roost completely covered in snow. The depression and droppings can sometimes be located.

Shallow depressions about 25 cm (10 in.) in diameter on old ant hills, or in sandy loam, show where grouse have taken a dust bath. If you look closely, you will find small feathers or down fluff mixed in the ground around the depression.

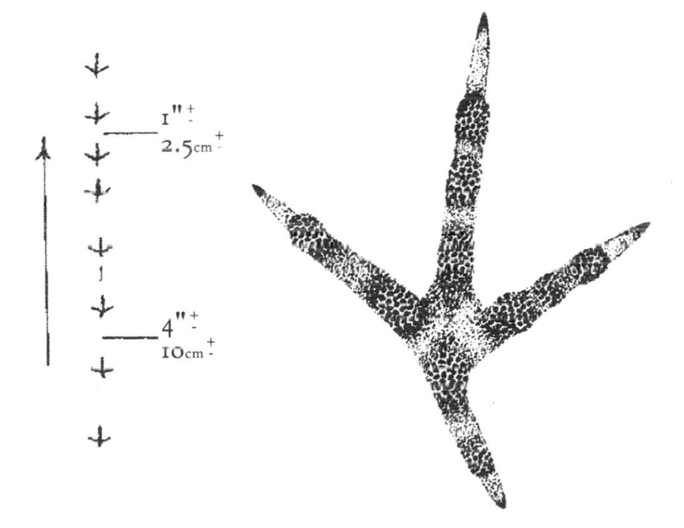

Herring Gull

Size

48–53cm (19"–21")

Colour

White, with black wing tips

Habitat

Saltwater coastal areas, ranging inland

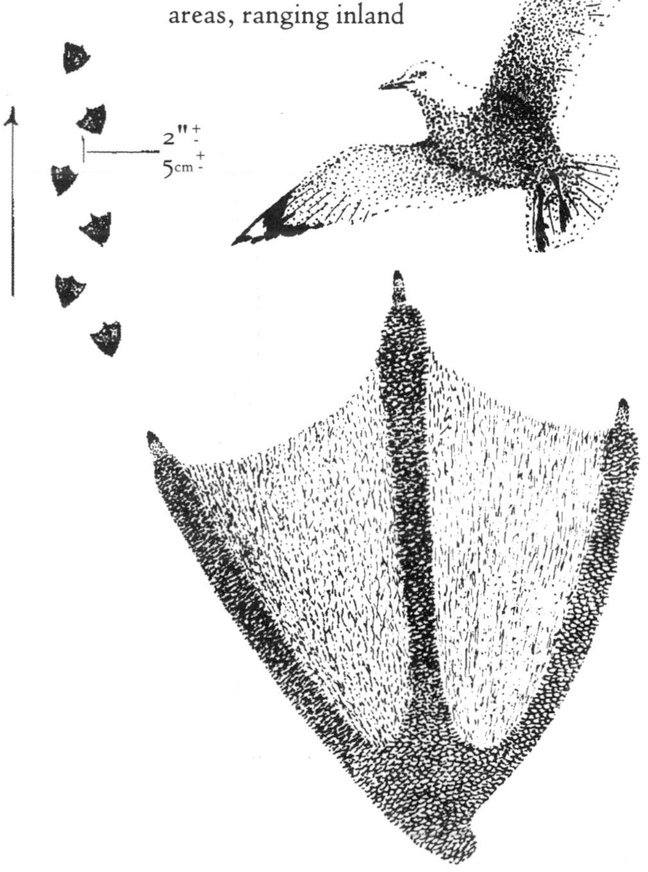

Rock Dove or Pigeon

Size

25.5–30.5cm (10"–12")

Colour

Slate grey with some black and white, some are brown with white

Habitat

Urban areas, expanding into rural areas. Nesting under highway bridges, rock crevices, in and around buildings.

Sparrow e.g. White-throated Sparrow

Size

16.5–18 cm (6½"– 7".)

Colour

Grey-breasted with white throat patch, striped black and white crown and yellow spot between bill and eye.

Habitat

Spruce forests.

Other Species

Birds of Prey

This group includes hawks, eagles, falcons, ospreys, owls and some gulls.

These birds all feed on the flesh of other animals. Some parts of these animals, such as leg bones or hair, are not digestible. The birds of prey digest what they can; the remainder is removed through regurgitation. The indigestible portion of the food is ejected from the stomach in the form of a pellet.

It is possible to mistake this pellet for scat. The pellet, however, is usually found beneath the roosting area. This could be an old dead tree or any high perch which would give a good view of the area below. Pellets are usually found one at a time unless the roost has been used over a period of time. Scat is commonly found in large numbers. The pellet when fresh appears to have a shiny mucus-like covering, which is not found on scat. Therefore the location, the number, and the appearance of the outer layer may help to identify a specimen as a pellet rather than scat.

References

Peterson Field Guides

Burt, W.H. and Grossenheider, R.P. *A Field Guide to the Mammals,* Boston, Houghton, Mifflin Co., 1964; reprinted 1976

Murie, O. *A Field Guide to Animal Tracks,* Boston, Houghton Mifflin Co., 1954; reprinted 1975

Peterson, R.T. *A Field Guide to the Birds,* Eastern Land and Water Birds, Boston, Houghton Mifflin Co., 1947; reprinted 1980

Other

Tufts, Robie W. *The Birds of Nova Scotia* Halifax, N.S., Nova Scotia Museum, 1986

Ormond, Clyde *Complete Book of Outdoor Lore* New York, Harper and Row, 1966

Banfield, A.W.F. *The Mammals of Canada* Toronto, University of Toronto Press, 1974

Notes on Nova Scotia Wildlife, Nova Scotia Department of Lands and Forests, 1980; reprinted 1987.

Wooding, Frederick H. *Wild Mammals of Canada* Toronto: McGraw Hill Ryerson, 1982.

Notes

NOTES

NOTES